North and South Korea

Cath Senker

First published in 2011 by Wayland

Wayland
338 Euston Road
London NW1 3BH

Wayland Australia
Level 17/207 Kent Street
Sydney, NSW 2000

Managing editor: Debbie Foy
Designer: Stephen Prosser
Picture researcher: Kathy Lockley
Maps: Ian Thompson

Picture Acknowledgments: The author and publisher would like to thank the following for allowing their pictures to be reproduced in this publication: Cover: Mika Heittola/Shuttertsock (top) and Lee Jae-Won/Reuters/Corbis (bottom); AFP/AFP/Getty Images: 26, 27; Nathan Benn/ Corbis: 14; Corbis: 9; EPA/Corbis: 22; Wu Hong/ EPA/Corbis: 18; Lee Jae-Won/Reuters/Corbis: 7; Lee Jin-man/AP/Press Association Images: Title page, 33; KeystoneUSA-ZUMA/Rex Features: 23, 38, 40; Peter Parks/AFP/Getty Images: 30 Jason Reed/Corbis: 25; RIA Novosti/TopFoto/ TopFoto.co.uk: 17,19, 21; Lucas Schifres/ Pictobank/ABACAPRESS.COM/Press Association Images: 31; Sipa Press/Rex Features: 13, 20, 29, 34, 37, 43; STR/AFP/Getty Images: 6, 42; Chung Sung-Jun/Getty Images: 28; TopFoto/ ImageWorks/Topfoto.co.uk: 32; TopFoto/ TopFoto.co.uk: 10, 11; Topham Picturepoint/ TopFoto.co.uk: 24; Jung Yeon-Je/AFP/Getty Images: 39; YONHAP/AFP/Getty Images: 15; Yonhap News Agency/EPA/Corbis: 36; Georgios Kollidas/Shutterstock.com: 12; Maxim Tupikov/ Shutterstock.com: 35; Narvikk/iStockphoto.com: 16

Should there be any inadvertent omission please apply to the publisher for rectification.

Acknowledgments:
The author would like to acknowledge the following sources of information for case studies: p6–7 A deadly attack: *North Korea: a deadly attack* by Tania Branigan and Ewen MacAskill, guardian.co.uk, 23 November 2010; p11 Tae-woo: severed from his family: *Nothing to Envy: Real Lives in North Korea* by Barbara Demick (Granta Books, 2010); p19 Dying of starvation: *North Korea Today Famine Special* by Good Friends (ReliefWeb, 1 May 2008); p27 Surviving a labour camp: Testimony of Ms. Soon Ok Lee (US Senate Committee on the Judiciary, 21 June 2002); p37 South Korea's anti-base movement: 'Anti-Base Movements in South Korea: Comparative Perspective on the Asia-Pacific', *The Asia-Pacific Journal*, 14 June 2010.

Should there be any inadvertent omission please apply to the publisher for rectification.

British Library Cataloguing in Publication Data:
North and South Korea. -- (Our world divided)
1. Korea (North)--Foreign relations--Korea (South)--
Juvenile literature. 2. Korea (South)--Foreign relations--
Korea (North)--Juvenile literature.
I. Series
327.5'19305195-dc22

ISBN: 978 0 7502 6584 3

Printed in China

Wayland is a division of Hachette Children's Books, an Hachette UK company.

www.hachette.co.uk

Contents

Chapter 1

A deadly attack

The residents of Yeonpyeong, a small island 120 km (75 miles) west of the South Korean capital Seoul, never expected to be at the centre of renewed conflict between North and South Korea. Yet on 23 November 2010, North Korean forces suddenly bombarded the island, firing around 200 shells. Two soldiers and two civilians (non-military) lost their lives, while at least 17 others were injured. Fifty-four-year-old Lee Chung-ok was watching TV when she heard artillery fire, and a wall and door in her home collapsed. 'I thought I would die,' she told journalists in a state of shock. Plumes of smoke rose from the houses as the shelling continued.

▲ ***Plumes of smoke rise from Yeonpyeong Island during the North Korean attack.***

The reaction was swift. The South Korean forces returned fire, and F-16 fighter jets were scrambled, ready to respond to any further bombardment. The islanders were rapidly evacuated to emergency shelters.

What prompted this unexpected attack? South Korea had been carrying out regular military exercises in the area, and it appeared that the North had objected to them. The assault occurred just days after the news that North Korea was pressing ahead with its nuclear programme. This serious escalation of tensions in the Korean peninsula sent shockwaves across the world. The international community called for restraint on both sides, but a week after the attack, the incoming South Korean defence minister vowed that if North

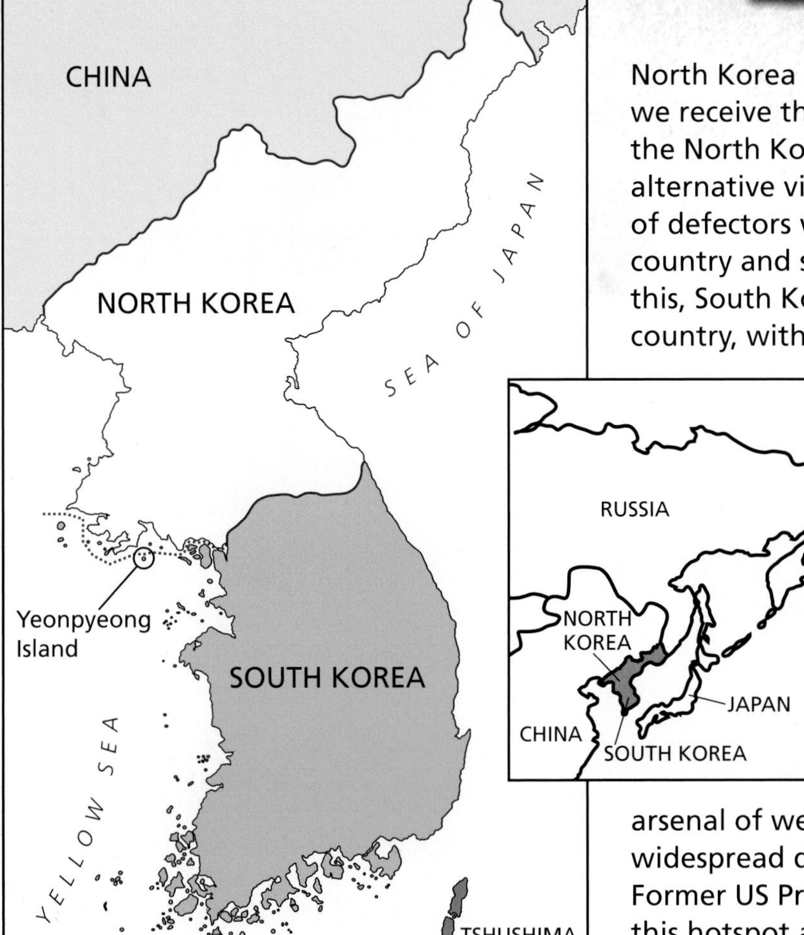

▲ ***The main map showing the location of Yeonpyeong Island, close to North Korea. The inset map showing the global position of North and South Korea.***

Korea provoked his country again, 'We will definitely use aircraft to attack North Korea'. Fears arose that the situation could spiral dangerously out of control.

Polar opposites

At the start of the 21st century, Korea is a divided country. No communication exists between the North and South; there is no postal or telephone service. Families separated by the border have no contact.

North Korea is a closed society. From outside, we receive the official viewpoint from the North Korean government; the only alternative views come from the tiny number of defectors who have escaped from the country and some aid agencies. In contrast to this, South Korea is a modern, industrialized country, with a Western-style democracy and free press. Information about South Korea is available from a wide variety of sources.

These two nations with totally different governments face each other across the demilitarized zone (DMZ). It is one of the most heavily defended frontiers in the world. On either side of the DMZ lies a vast arsenal of weapons that, if used, would cause widespread destruction across the region. Former US President Bill Clinton described this hotspot as the 'scariest place on earth'. This book explores the historical, economic, social and military divisions in Korea and presents a variety of opinions for debate.

▲ ***The DMZ is still heavily guarded today.***

Chapter 2

History: a country torn in two

Korea is an East Asian territory. Over history, it has frequently been invaded. In 1905, the Japanese conquered Korea and ruled it until their defeat at the end of World War II in 1945. Korea was then divided into two zones, which laid the ground for its partition into separate states.

Creating the divide

In August 1945, once it became clear that Japan had lost World War II in East Asia, the USA decreed that the Japanese would surrender to the Soviet forces north of the 38th parallel (see map page 9). In the south, they would surrender to US forces.

The Soviet army marched into the north with Korean Communists who had been living in the Soviet Union (USSR). Communist leader Kim Il-sung established himself as the leader of North Korea, with the support of the USSR. In 1947, the United Nations (UN) discussed the reunification of Korea. It adopted a resolution that called for elections to a National Assembly to create a government. However, the Soviet Union did not accept the plan. Elections took place in 1948 in the South alone, and Syngman Rhee was elected president. The Republic of Korea was formed, with Seoul as the capital. The UN accepted it as the sole lawful government of Korea.

Meanwhile, in the North, the Communist Democratic People's Republic of Korea was proclaimed in September 1948, with Kim Il-sung as premier and the capital in Pyongyang. The USSR recognized Kim Il-sung's regime as the only legal government of Korea, and so Korea was partitioned. The Korean people were angered by the unnatural division of their country. They felt they were like 'shrimp among whales', powerless against the superpowers that had decided their fate.

The Cold War

After World War II, friction developed between the two superpowers, the USA and the USSR. Each tried to gain influence over other countries to expand their power. This became known as the Cold War. Korea became a focus of the struggle, with Communist China backing its North Korean ally and the USA supporting South Korea.

The Korean War 1950–53

Kim Il-sung was determined to reunite Korea under his rule. The USSR helped to establish the North Korean army. Although the USA backed South Korea with economic and military aid, by 1950, the North Korean forces were far stronger than those of the South. In June, the Communist troops invaded South Korea and overwhelmed its army. The UN sent in forces to try to repel the North Koreans; the USA supplied most

▲ ***US forces fighting in the Korean War.***

of the troops and equipment. The UN almost succeeded in taking the entire peninsula, but then in October 1950, China entered the war to back North Korea. The conflict continued until a ceasefire was agreed in 1953. Nearly four million people had died. Under the armistice (ceasefire) agreement, the boundary between the two states was fixed further north than the 38th parallel. Each force pulled back 2 km (1.2 miles) to create a demilitarized zone.

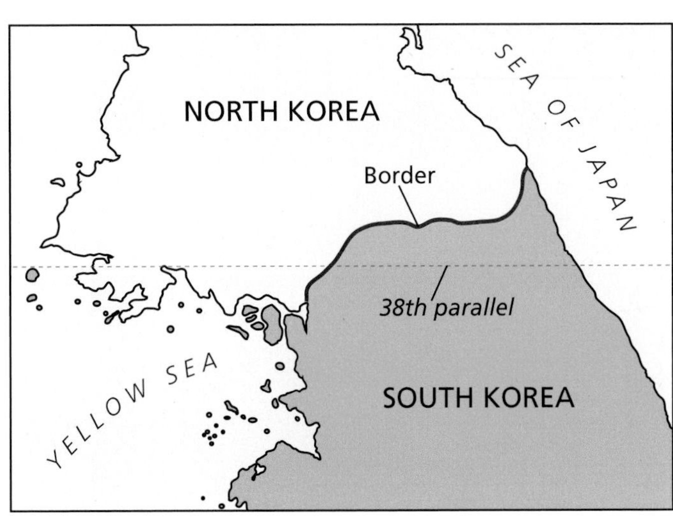

▲ ***This map shows North and South Korea, with the border created after the Korean War.***

Although there was an armistice, no peace agreement was made, so the two Koreas are technically still at war. Tensions have existed ever since. Following the Korean War, the USA reinforced South Korea's military forces with ground troops, naval forces in the Pacific Ocean and its own nuclear deterrent (defence system). On the other side of the divide, North Korea poured a huge proportion of its resources into creating a large army.

North Korea: strict Communism

The political system in North Korea was modelled on Soviet-style Communism. The state owned all the means of production. Agriculture was collectivized – farmers worked together on the land and gave the produce to the government, which supplied cheap food and clothing to the people. The government focused on setting up state-owned industries. It developed economic plans to fix the targets.

In the 1950s, North Korea received subsidized (cheap) food and other goods from Communist countries, which enabled it to implement its economic development plans. During the 1960s, North Koreans were generally better off than their southern counterparts. Everyone had shelter and clothing, and by 1970 every village was wired up for electricity. However, in the late 1960s, Kim Il-sung decided to focus on expanding the army and military facilities to protect the country against outside threats. This absorbed a large part of the country's resources.

Women doing military training in North Korea, 1960.

Case Study

Tae-woo: severed from his family

Born in South Korea in 1932, Tae-woo was 18 when the Communists invaded his country. Although his father had died and he was the family's breadwinner, Tae-woo was forced to enlist in the army. His last battle took place in July 1953 in the North. Tae-woo's unit was surrounded by Chinese soldiers; he and about 500 others were taken as prisoners of war (POWs) and detained in squalid conditions.

▲ *A prisoner about to be sent back to North Korea, 1953.*

After the armistice, a prisoner exchange took place. Along with many others, Tae-woo was loaded on to a train at Pyongyang station. He hoped he was going home. Yet instead, he was sent north to the mines, where he was forced to labour in dirty, dangerous conditions. In 1956, the South Korean POWs received North Korean citizenship. Tae-woo would never be able to return to his family.

While working at an iron-ore mine in Musan, Tae-woo met and married a North Korean woman and settled down to his new life. It was easy to blend in – after all, North and South Koreans were one people. However, Tae-woo's history as an enemy soldier gave him a low ranking in North Korean society. He would never live in a pleasant area of the country or hold a good job. Furthermore, his children would carry his 'tainted blood' and their horizons would be similarly limited.

Following the leader

State-controlled economic development and a strong army were key to *juche*, the North Korean version of Communism. It was adopted as the official state ideology (set of ideas) in 1972. According to *juche*, North Korea aimed to develop in its own way rather than blindly following other countries' methods. Korean Communism was combined with a strong leadership cult; Kim Il-sung was seen as the father of the nation and worshipped by the population. For instance, all North Koreans had to keep a portrait of him hanging on the wall at home; inspectors checked every month to ensure the portrait was kept clean.

Viewpoints

'Establishing *juche* means, in a nutshell, being the master of revolution and reconstruction in one's own country. This means holding fast to an independent position, rejecting dependence on others . . . displaying the revolutionary spirit of self-reliance.'

Kim Il-sung, undated

'Critics say [*juche*] is a sham ideology that only serves to harden the grip of the North Korean leadership on the people of the country by creating an illusion of constant outside aggression and deflects attention from the reality that [the] Pyongyang [government] depends on outside assistance to feed its people.'

Jaeyeon Woo, 26 January 2011

▲ ***Kim Il-sung's portrait on a North Korean banknote, 1978.***

• Kim Il-sung, former leader of North Korea, explains the idea of *juche*.

• Jaeyeon Woo, a journalist for the US newspaper, the *Wall Street Journal*, summarizes the critics' view of *juche*.

• Consider the different motives of the two writers.

Collapse into crisis

During the 1970s, the economy began to falter. North Korea received less aid from Communist countries, yet maintained high levels of spending on the military and heavy industry. This led to food shortages, exacerbated by the increase in the population, which soared threefold from 1953 to 1993. The situation grew worse in the following decade. After Communism collapsed in the Soviet Union and Eastern Europe at the end of the 1980s, North Korea lost support and trading partners. It now focused on developing nuclear weapons, which drained its economic resources even further.

Additional crises hit in the 1990s. The death of Kim Il-sung in 1994 caused initial shock, but his son Kim Jong-Il was able to maintain the same political system. During this decade, droughts and floods added to economic woes, leading to starvation on a mass scale. Staple crops were still grown on collective farms and taken by the state, but the government provided ever-smaller amounts of food. Therefore farmers tended to neglect the collective farms. They focused on growing their own vegetables in kitchen gardens to provide for their families. In urban areas, people had no land and they struggled to survive. It is estimated that up to two million people died of starvation in the 1990s.

▼ ***A farmer and his calf work the fields during the North Korean famine, 1999.***

South Korea: the road to democracy

After the Korean War, South Korea had an authoritarian government; the power lay in one strong leader. Dissatisfaction with the government grew in 1960, and it could no longer maintain law and order. In 1961 General Park Chung-hee led a military coup, and the army ruled until 1987, when former army general Roh Tae Woo won the election. He worked to re-establish democracy, and in 1992 Kim Young-sam became the first civilian (non-military) president.

An economic miracle

From the early 1960s, the government transformed the economy, with US aid. Over the next 30 years, income per person rose by an astounding hundredfold. Firstly, light manufacturing industries were established, then heavy industries in the 1970s. In the following decade, South Korea shifted to hi-tech manufacturing, producing cars and electronic goods. Government policies promoted a well-educated and highly skilled workforce. They supported the development of *chaebol* (giant global companies), such as Hyundai and Samsung, which achieved global success and became household names.

The 'sunshine policy'

During the late 1990s, South Korea embarked on the 'sunshine policy' to improve relations with North Korea. It provided aid, such as fertilizers and rice,

▲ *A worker on an assembly line in a South Korean car factory, 1987.*

and encouraged economic co-operation; for example, South Korean businesses employed North Koreans at Kaesong industrial complex (see page 20). In 2000, a landmark summit took place between the leaders of the two states. They agreed that South Korea would invest in the North, they would work towards reuniting families separated by the Korean War and would aim to reunify the country. However, South Korean president Lee Myung-bak ended the 'sunshine policy' in 2008. He believed in a tougher approach to North Korea.

As of 2011, South Korea was the 13th richest country in the world, while its enemy across the border was the 98th.

▲ ***The North and South Korean leaders at the 2000 summit.***

What does 'sunshine policy' mean?

The term 'sunshine policy' comes from one of Aesop's Fables. The Sun and the Wind compete to see who can strip the clothes off a traveller:

'The North Wind tried first. He blew violently. As the man clung to his clothes, the North Wind attacked him with greater force. But the man, uncomfortable from the cold, put on more clothes.

The Sun now shone moderately, and the man removed his extra outer cloak. Then the sun darted beams which were more scorching until the man . . . took off his clothes.'

The story shows that it is easier to encourage a person to change something himself than to force him to do it. (Quoted in *Korea*, Christopher Bluth, 2008)

Conflict in Korea: key events

1945 Korea is divided into two zones.

1948 The Republic of Korea is formed in the South while the Democratic People's Republic of Korea is declared in the North.

1950–53 The Korean War is fought.

Late 1990s–2008 South Korea's 'sunshine policy' promotes co-operation between the enemy states.

March 2010 North Korea sinks a South Korean naval ship, the *Cheonan*, killing 46 sailors.

November 2010 North Korea attacks Yeonpyeong, South Korea.

Chapter 3

Poverty-stricken North vs wealthy South

The economies of North and South Korea are founded on completely different models, and the difference in their economic situation is vast. North Korea is extremely poor, with industry and agriculture in long-term decline. In total contrast, South Korea has a highly industrialized Western-style capitalist economy.

▲ *Kim Il-sung Square in Pyongyang. The modern buildings and vehicles indicate that life is better here than in rural areas.*

Industry in North Korea

The state controls all the factories and land in North Korea – there are no legal private companies. Since the collapse of the economy in the 1990s, the crisis has become so severe that there is little electricity production. Many heavy industries are unable to operate, and the machinery lies idle. Of the existing production, most is geared towards the military. North Korea possesses important minerals, including iron ore, coal and gold, but the lack of electricity has affected the mining industry, too.

Food and farming

Only 16 per cent of the land in North Korea is suitable for farming. The collective farms have proved to be inefficient (see page 13). Farmers also suffer from a great scarcity of grain, fertilizers and machinery. North Korea has to import food – even rice, a staple food – to make up for the shortfall in production. In the early 21st century, food shortages remain a serious economic problem.

Owing to the collective farming system, people receive food rations. The top tiers of society, the Communist Party, the military, the residents of Pyongyang and defence industry workers, are assured sufficient food. Yet around 60 per cent of the population, the ordinary workers and farmers, receive few rations. During the famine conditions of the 1990s, desperate North Koreans developed a black market to try to survive. Food grown in farmers' private plots or smuggled in from China was sold in illegal markets. Since the production of consumer goods such as clothes and household goods has always been a low priority in North Korea, these items were also smuggled into the country from China and Japan and sold on the black market.

▲ ***This North Korean farmer uses a buffalo to pull his cart; he has no machinery.***

New markets flourish

In 2002 the regime was forced to relent and legalized markets to allow trade to take place. Middle-aged women are the most active traders; they are prepared to work long hours to supplement the family income. The markets provide a greater availability of goods for those who can afford them, including food, Western-style clothing (especially popular with young people) and mass-produced items such as notebooks and ballpoint pens.

Fact panel	North Korea	South Korea
Population	22.8 million	48.6 million
Capital	Pyongyang	Seoul
Area	121,000 sq km	99,700 sq km
Language	Korean	Korean
Main religions	Traditionally Buddhist, Confucianist and Christian but no religious freedom	Christianity and Buddhism; 49 per cent no religion
Life expectancy	64	79
Gross Domestic Product (GDP) per head	US$1,800	US$30,000
Currency	North Korean won	South Korean won

▲ *These North Korean women work long hours selling seafood at a market.*

Clampdown on traders

The markets allowed people to buy much-needed goods but also encouraged the import of banned products, such as films from South Korea. In May 2009 the government decided to punish traders by imposing price controls on non-food basic items sold in the markets, such as toothbrushes, spoons and candles. In November, it devalued the currency by one hundred times with virtually no advance notice, and brought in a new currency: 1,000 won in the old currency were now worth just 10 won! Citizens were permitted to exchange only 100,000 won (US$25–30) into the new currency. Many people's entire savings were lost overnight and they could no longer engage in business. After this disastrous move, the markets gradually revived, but prices soared.

The 'second economy'

Nowadays, nearly every household is involved in some kind of market activity. In towns people have to earn money in the markets to be able to buy food. In both legal and black markets, around 70 to 80 per cent of the goods are Chinese products, distributed by trade companies or smugglers. The rest are from North Korean factories, collective farms, private households, underground factories and stolen materials. The underground factories are illegal small private enterprises where people work for wages to make consumer goods. They form part of the unofficial private 'second economy'.

The prices in the private markets are far higher than the government-fixed prices for rationed food – since 2004 they have been 10 to 40 times higher. In 2008, prices rose so high in several provinces that some people who could not afford to buy sufficient food died from starvation. Nevertheless, the market economy has allowed North Korea to avoid the mass starvation of the 1990s.

Case Study

Dying of starvation

Between January and May 2008, there was a serious shortage of food rations in the southern provinces of North Korea, while the price of rice and maize rocketed. Many families were surviving on just one meal a day, eating noodles, porridge, grass or mountain greens boiled with salt. The poorest ate nothing but a thin, watery maize porridge that offered no nutrition. Some people were so weak that they could no longer move their bodies and became painfully thin. Dangerously weakened, they easily fell prey to disease. In May, one or two people were dying every day in each district in North Hwanghae province. Officials from the Communist Party could offer no practical help. In Yangduk, South Pyongan Province, they said, 'All of us are facing difficult times, so let's tighten our belts and solve this problem. Everyone report to work'. Farmer Han Kyung-duk replied, 'Please give us something to eat. We need to eat something in order to have the strength to work'.

In desperation, North Korea sought food aid from international aid agencies and the USA to avert widespread deaths.

These residents of the North Korean city of Najin fetch wood to use as fuel.

Reluctant contact with the outside world

Despite the principle of *juche*, North Korea was forced to seek foreign aid in the 1990s because of its dire economic circumstances. The USA, Japan and South Korea remain the main sources of aid.

Under pressure, the government also began to encourage foreign investment. In 2002, it even allowed South Korean businesses to establish some industries in the Kaesong Industrial Complex in the south-west, employing North Korean workers. The country has also opened up a little to tourism, allowing visitors to travel to the sightseeing areas around Mount Kumgang, in the south-east. The government maintains strict supervision of these enterprises, which are intended to make money for North Korea rather than to promote contact with the outside world.

▲ ***A bus brings South Korean tourists back from Mount Kumgang.***

North Korea has also expanded international trade. Its main trading partners are China, South Korea, Russia, Japan and Thailand. It mostly imports food, drinks and other agricultural products, and exports live animals, textiles, clothing, machinery and mineral fuels.

USA punishes North Korea

Not all international contact has brought positive effects. Since the 1990s, the USA has regularly imposed financial sanctions on North Korea to discourage it from developing nuclear weapons. The sanctions prevent trade with the USA. The US government hoped that this measure would cut off North Korea's income for producing these expensive weapons (see page 32). However, the sanctions have not hit the nuclear programme, but have affected the economy. Foreign businesspeople and diplomats in Pyongyang have claimed that the banking sanctions have blocked the legal imports of industrial equipment for the production of consumer goods and slowed down economic growth.

Viewpoints

'Sliced vegetables preserved in soy sauce, traditional Korean food, are everyday dishes for the Koreans. They are made of agricultural produce and meat. . . . The Sariwon Jongbang Foodstuff Producers' Cooperative and other foodstuff producers across the country are preserving sliced cucumbers, radishes, broad bellflowers, mushrooms, etc. in soy sauce and supplying them to working people.'

Korean News, 14 February 2011

'Reports of deaths from starvation surfaced in the months following North Korea's ineptly managed monetary devaluation scheme. . . . South Korea-based NGOs [non-governmental organizations] and media with informants inside North Korea reported on new hunger-related deaths, especially among vulnerable groups. . . . Although several international humanitarian agencies [organizations that reduce suffering] continued to deliver food and services, they have continued to have difficulty confirming delivery to the most needy.'

Human Rights Watch 'World Report 2011: North Korea'

- The official North Korean news agency depicts the view that agricultural co-operatives are handing out delicious food to the people.
- Human Rights Watch is an independent organization devoted to defending human rights.
- Consider the motives of the people who supplied the information in each quote.

◀ ***Farmers working on a collective farm outside Najin. These farms do not provide enough food.***

South Korea: an Asian tiger

Due to its powerful economic growth, South Korea was named an 'Asian tiger' economy in 2010. It had the fourth largest economy in Asia and the 13th largest in the world. Since the 1980s, the country has invested in hi-tech industries, such as vehicle manufacturing, electronic equipment, bio-engineering and aerospace (building aircraft and satellites). Information technology has become increasingly significant to economic growth.

South Korea is a world leader in digital technology, in great contrast with its northern neighbour, one of the countries with the least modern equipment globally (see page 26). Most people have digital cable and satellite and by 2009 nearly 37.5 million Koreans (out of a population of around 48 million) were online. The country has pioneered TV via mobile devices and the Internet.

Unlike North Korea, South Korea has a growing service industry (industries providing a service, for example, shops, offices and transport), occupying one-fifth of the labour force. Tourism makes a major contribution to the country's income. The agriculture sector is far more productive than in North Korea, with high levels of rice production.

However, the downside of South Korea's economic miracle is that inequality has

▲ *A South Korean watches a portable television that can be used anywhere in her home.*

grown between the richest groups that benefit the most from these new opportunities, and the poorest.

Neighbourly relations

South Korea's foreign policy is the opposite of *juche*; it welcomes close relationships with other countries. It trades in the region with Japan and South-east Asian countries, while its main international trading partners are the USA and the European Union. South Korea is a member of the G20 group of economically powerful nations, and its president, Lee Myung-bak, chaired the G20 in 2010. While North Korea follows its own individual path and is seen by the international community as a 'rogue state', South Korea holds power and influence in the global arena.

▲ ***US President Barack Obama with Lee Myung-bak at the G20 summit in 2010.***

Viewpoints:

'Money paid to North Korean workers at the [Kaesong] industrial park amounts to mere billions of won, but the value of the enterprise is far greater when you consider how it contributes to the lessening of tensions and the increase in economic exchange.'

Hankyoreh

'Pyongyang's recent brinkmanship has . . . caused a profound shift in public opinion . . . that reflects a less sympathetic, more aggressive state of mind. . . . [T]here are . . . signs that the public is less willing to send aid to North Korea if the receiving nation doesn't show greater signs of reciprocity [giving something in return].'

Gregory Rodriguez

- The progressive South Korean newspaper *Hankyoreh* argues that aid to North Korea is the best way to improve its economy and reduce tensions between the two Koreas.

- Gregory Rodriguez, a member of the public policy organization, the New American Foundation, believes that after North Korea test-fired missiles in the Sea of Japan in 2006, many South Koreans became less keen to assist their neighbour.

- Should South Korea offer aid to North Korea, or only if the country makes reforms?

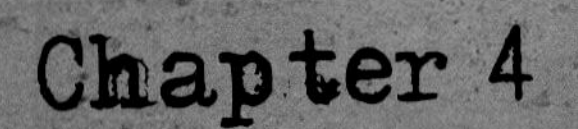

Chapter 4
Western freedoms vs a secretive society

Koreans are one people but over 60 years, the markedly different governments of the North and South have created two contrasting societies. North Korea lacks democracy and human rights while South Korea is an open, democratic country.

Life in North Korea

In North Korea, the jobs people can do depend on their rank in society. According to Communist principles, everyone should have equal opportunities in life. Yet North Korean society is divided into tiers. The top tier consists of the senior Communist Party members and military leaders. They receive a privileged education and have the best jobs in the government and the army. The residents of the capital Pyongyang form the next tier. This group enjoys a relatively high standard of living and consumer goods that people in lower tiers cannot obtain. The members of the third tier, mostly defence workers, receive more benefits than ordinary people.

Residents of Pyongyang receive better rations than other North Koreans.

The majority of people in the fourth tier are workers, farmers and minor officials. These groups work in industry, mining or agriculture. It is normal to work long hours, six days a week. At the very bottom are those descended from enemies of the government or relatives of people who have escaped from North Korea, who undertake the dirtiest and most dangerous jobs. It is extraordinarily hard for people with a 'tainted' family background to progress in society. Even if they are extremely able academically, they are denied access to higher education.

At home

After work, most North Koreans return to simple, one-room homes in single-storey buildings, called 'harmonicas' (they resemble the tightly packed air slots of a harmonica). Owing to the electricity shortages, their homes are often dark. When night falls, people go to bed. Without lights – candles are expensive – they cannot even read books. North Koreans have little free time anyway. All are expected to attend regular political meetings in the evening to reinforce their loyalty to the regime. When they do have a day off, it is hard to travel, except on foot or by bicycle. Cars are rare, and the fuel crisis has severely reduced the running of public transport. For the majority, life is simply a daily struggle for survival.

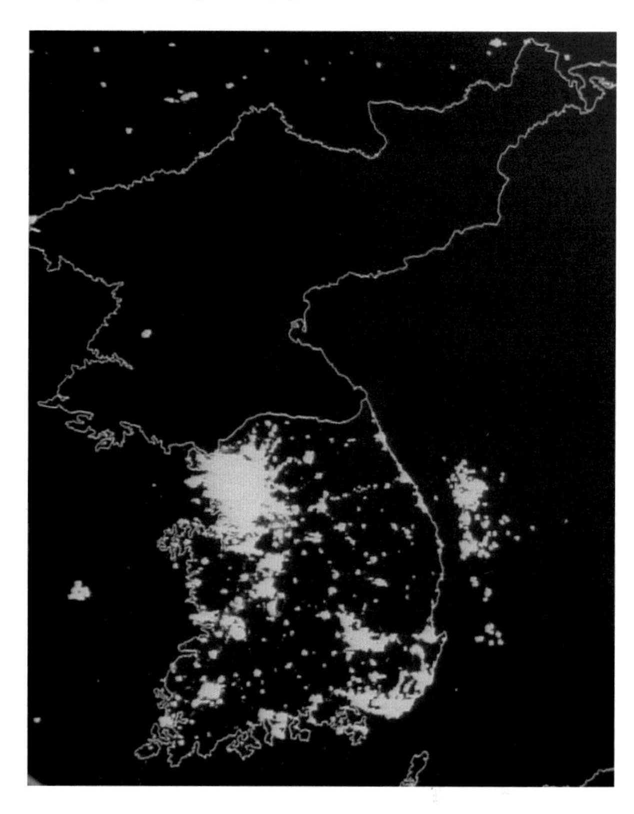

▲ ***This satellite image shows complete darkness in North Korea at night, 2006.***

Women: discrimination and hard work

North Korean women tend to work in lower-paid jobs, for example in light industry rather than the higher-paid heavy industrial jobs, undertaken by men. In offices, they work as secretaries and in other low-status posts. Mothers with young children go out to work every day, while their infants go to day-care centres. As well as working outside the home, women do most of the housework and cooking. Without the assistance of modern appliances such as washing machines and electric cookers, the daily tasks of cooking, washing and housework are extremely time-consuming.

Media and censorship

North Korea is a closed society with no freedom of expression. The government tightly controls the media, which presents propaganda informing citizens that they have a caring leader and nothing to envy in the world outside. A few privileged students are trained to become actors to act in propaganda films for the regime, the only movies that are legally shown. It is difficult to find independent information. Some officials have Internet access but it is denied to the general public. Foreign books are heavily censored or banned. Even communications within the country are difficult. The postal service is slow and there are few landline telephones or mobiles.

Spies in every neighbourhood

As well as using the media, the regime controls the people through a widespread network of spies. In every community, the inhabitants are organized into *inminban* – people's groups with an elected leader who run the neighbourhood and spy on each other. The leader, usually a middle-aged woman, reports any suspicious activity or rule breaking to an official. Offences include using more than the quota of electricity, complaining about the food situation, not showing proper respect to the leader, or illegally listening to a foreign broadcast. People denounce their neighbours and children report their parents for any criticism of the regime. Those who break the rules are banished to labour camps. The majority remain faithful to the system. Fearing arrest, they do not dare to complain.

▼ ***A North Korean television shot shows a parade to support the government.***

Case Study

Surviving a labour camp

▲ *This North Korean video shot supposedly shows prisoners going to a public trial, then to be executed.*

In 1984 Ms Soon Ok Lee was arrested under the false charge of stealing state property. She was subjected to severe torture during a 14-month investigation until she admitted to the charge and was sent to a labour camp. She describes the life of the prisoners – referred to by the guards as 'tailless beasts' because they did not consider them human: 'A prisoner has no right to talk, laugh, sing or look in a mirror. Prisoners must kneel down on the ground and keep their heads down deeply whenever called by a guard, they can say nothing except to answer questions asked. Women prisoners' babies are killed on delivery birth . Prisoners have to work as slaves for 18 hours daily.

Repeated failure to meet the work quotas means a week's time in a punishment cell. A prisoner must give up her human worth. When I was released, some 6,000 prisoners, both men and women, were crying and pleading with me in their hearts to let the outside world know of their suffering. How can I ever forget their eyes, the eyes of the tailless beasts?'

Ms Lee was fortunate to be released in a surprise amnesty (prisoner release) after five years and was able to escape the country.

Living in South Korea

In contrast, South Koreans can express their views publicly; media reporters frequently criticize the government. Most adults read a daily newspaper and are well informed about events in their country and the world.

Healthy and well educated

South Korea enjoys a high standard of education and healthcare. The government provides basic social welfare services, such as pensions and health insurance. Education is a high priority for families. Nearly all children complete high school. To enter university they have to undertake arduous preparation, memorizing a huge number of facts, in order to take fiercely competitive entrance exams. This is an extremely stressful experience! Attending a prestigious university is the best route to a good job.

Hard workers

South Koreans work hard like their northern neighbours. The country has one of the longest working weeks in the world. Although the law states that 40 hours is the maximum working week, many people regularly work several hours of overtime as well.

Free time

South Koreans do have some spare time to take part in leisure activities, many of which are the same as Western pastimes. They love sport: the martial art *tae kwon do* is popular, as are baseball and football. Outdoor pursuits are also greatly enjoyed; large numbers go hiking, camping and skiing in the country's national parks.

▲ ***Students sit the entrance exam for South Korea's top universities.***

▲ *Children practising the martial art* tae kwon do *in the open air.*

Modern yet traditional

South Korea has modernized rapidly, yet cultural traditions remain important. The family is the foundation of society and there is a strong sense of community. Unlike North Korea, it is easy to travel to visit relatives. The South has a well-developed transport network, with express highways linking most major cities, long-distance express buses and high-speed railway lines. Although it is common to move away from home for study and work, relatives regularly gather to celebrate important festivals, such as *Sollal*, the Lunar New Year and *Chusok*, the harvest-moon festival.

South Koreans have kept their traditional dietary habits, despite the introduction of a Western-style economy. The food scarcities of North Korea do not exist here. Most people continue to eat a diet based on rice and vegetables; pickled vegetables, known as *kimchi*, are a speciality.

Education fever in South Korea

- 15-year-olds in South Korea rank second in the world in reading and fourth in maths.
- The average South Korean family spends more than 10 per cent of its income on after-hours private tuition for their children.
- About 70 per cent of high school graduates go on to colleges; around half go to university.
- There are not enough jobs for all the graduates leaving university. Around 8 per cent of people under 30 are unemployed, more than twice the average unemployment rate.

Contacts beyond the peninsula

North Koreans are denied freedom of movement. A small number of businesspeople travel abroad for work purposes. If they fail to return, their families are sent to labour camps in punishment. However, since the 1990s, the deep poverty in North Korea and contrasting vibrant economic growth in neighbouring China have prompted North Koreans to risk escape. They seek the narrowest routes across the Tumen River and swim over to China, or walk across the ice in winter. If the Chinese authorities catch the defectors, they send them back to North Korea.

As North Koreans slip into China, black-market goods flow the other way. Smugglers bring food, clothes, books, radios, magazines and pirated DVDs; South Korean soap operas and comedies prove especially popular. Through these media, North Koreans learn about the outside world.

South Koreans: freedom to travel

Unlike their northern counterparts, South Koreans are free to travel and some emigrate, especially to the USA, Canada, Russia, China and Japan, while large numbers study abroad. The country has particularly close cultural ties with the USA, and American influences are strong. Yet South Koreans have virtually no contact with North Korea, the other part of their own country.

▲ ***A woman walks past a stall selling North Korean souvenirs in a Chinese town by the Tumen River.***

Viewpoints:

'... refusing to take up the issue [of human rights] has won no concessions from North Korea. On the contrary, engagement without even the strings of human decency attached serves only to persuade the North's Kim Jong-il that he can get away with anything, and that he has South Korea's government in his pocket, along with all the food, fertiliser . . . and other goodies it offers.'

The Economist, UK, 15 January 2005

'Concerns raised and recommendations made by participating States [in the Human Rights Council] included the right to food; lack of freedom of movement, opinion, expression and religious belief; the use of torture and other ill-treatment in detention facilities; the death penalty; abductions [taking away people illegally] and enforced disappearances. . . . Amnesty International calls on the North Korean authorities to specify to the Council at the earliest opportunity which recommendations it supports and to establish a national plan of action.'

Amnesty International Letter to Pak Ui-chu, the North Korean Minister for Foreign Affairs, 4 October 2010

▲ ***The Tumen River, the shallow, narrow border between China and North Korea.***

• The first article, from a respected British magazine, argues that South Korea should insist on improvements to human rights in North Korea in return for offering aid.

• The international human rights organization Amnesty International notes North Korea's human rights abuses and requests that it addresses them. It tries to put pressure directly on the North Korean government to allow more freedom.

• Which approach do you think is likely to be more successful?

Chapter 5

Armed and dangerous: the military build-up

Lethal forces are amassed in the Korean peninsula – conventional armies as well as chemical and nuclear weapons. In North Korea, the defence budget takes up an enormous 25 per cent of the country's GDP, while the powerful USA provides support to the South Korean army. Each country fears attack by the other. Is there a real threat to peace in the region today?

Rival armies

North Korea's armed forces number nearly 1.2 million soldiers on active duty and the army can call on more than 7 million reserves. Its army is twice the size of that of South Korea. However, South Korea has state-of-the-art equipment, including faster tanks with greater firepower. North Korea's tanks use outdated 1970s technology. The South Korean army's superior training and equipment give it the edge over its northern rival. It is also backed by US forces within the country, and if a confrontation occurred, the USA would immediately send further military reinforcements.

▲ ***South Korean soldiers patrol the border with North Korea.***

The nuclear threat

North Korea has prioritized the development of nuclear weapons; its first nuclear reactor began operation in Yongbyon in 1986. The country proved it is developing nuclear weapons when it exploded its first nuclear bomb in a test in October 2006. In May 2009, North Korea carried out a second nuclear test. However, most experts believed that the country had not yet produced a missile that could carry a nuclear warhead; they suggested it would take North Korea at least a decade to achieve this. On the other side, South Korea no longer has its own nuclear programme but in December 2010 was considering allowing the return of US tactical nuclear weapons to boost its defences.

▲ *South Koreans protest against North Korea's nuclear test, May 2009.*

In the 'axis of evil'

As well as raising tensions on the Korean peninsula, North Korea has been accused of sponsoring terrorism abroad. There is evidence that it has provided military equipment to nations that supported terrorist groups in the early 2000s, such as Libya and Syria. This has angered the international community, especially the USA. In 2002 then US President George W. Bush included North Korea in a list of countries he considered to form an 'axis of evil'. However, some experts argue that North Korea has not actively supported terrorists for decades and is unlikely to sell nuclear weapons to them for fear of retaliation.

North Korea's toxic threat

While no precise statistics are available, experts believe that North Korea has a vast stockpile of chemical weapons, somewhere between 2,500 and 5,000 tonnes. It is reported that they include agents that cause choking (phosgene), blistering (mustard gas), nerve damage (sarin) and blood poisoning (hydrogen cyanide).

Why does North Korea have huge military power?

It could be argued that North Korea acts defensively. The North Korean government is suspicious of the outside world and perceives many serious threats from other powers. As an isolated country, it maintains a large army and nuclear weapons to deter an attack by the USA or South Korea. Perhaps this has worked; the USA seems reluctant to target North Korea because of the destructive effects of nuclear conflict.

Indeed, the serious consequences make it even more unlikely that North Korea would resort to launching nuclear weapons. Clearly a nuclear strike would have a devastating impact on the South and would lead to swift retaliation by the USA, which could destroy both Koreas. Therefore, it could be that North Korea sees the weapons as a political tool, a bargaining chip in negotiations to ensure the regime's survival.

The Six-Party Talks

Other countries have attempted to negotiate with North Korea to halt the further development of nuclear weapons. In 2003 the Six-Party Talks began, involving North and South Korea, China, the USA, Russia and Japan. Yet, in April 2009, North Korea pulled out of the talks.

▲ *The leaders of the six nations at the Six-Party Talks in 2003.*

Viewpoints:

'While on the one hand it is claimed that missiles and nuclear weapons are designed to deter an American attack, on the other hand the fact that North Korea appears to be willing to bargain them away against political assurances and economic support seems to raise the question of their military significance in the first place.'

Christoph Bluth, 2008

'The United States and other members of the United Nations Security Council, which are so strong in their condemnation of North Korea's nuclear testing, are not doing enough to resolve important security issues with North Korea by diplomacy, the only sensible solution. Nor are the permanent members of the Security Council setting the right example by adhering [sticking] to their own obligations under international law for "good faith" negotiations for total nuclear disarmament [dismantling nuclear weapons].'

David Krieger, President, Nuclear Age Peace Foundation, 28 May 2009

- Bluth is a Professor of International Studies at the University of Leeds, UK. He thinks that North Korea might be using its nuclear weapons programme as a bargaining tool.
- Krieger believes that diplomacy is the way to resolve the conflict and that no country should have nuclear weapons.
- Should North Korea be allowed nuclear weapons or not?

North Korean armed forces on parade in Pyongyang in 2008.

North Korea's nuclear weapons

January 1986 The first nuclear reactor starts operation.

October 2002 North Korea admits that it has a programme to produce highly enriched uranium (HEU), which is needed for nuclear weapons.

October 2006 North Korea tests a nuclear bomb.

May 2009 North Korea carries out a second nuclear test.

January 2011 A report to the UN states that North Korea has undeclared uranium enrichment facilities.

Should South Korea rely on the USA?

To defend his country from its volatile neighbour, President Lee Myung-bak favours a strong alliance with the USA and a tough stance towards North Korea. The US maintains 37,000 troops in South Korea to help to defend it against the North. In 2007 it was agreed that the USA would withdraw these forces in 2012. In 2010, owing to rising tensions, this date was put back to 2015. Yet although the government welcomes American involvement, debate rages among South Koreans over the presence of US troops.

Those who approve of the US forces argue that North Korea poses a dangerous threat, that the American contribution to South Korea's armed forces remains significant and that a powerful US–South Korean alliance is the best deterrent. Opponents contend that South Korea is a wealthy country that can easily protect itself from isolated North Korea.

North Korea attacks: a divided response

In 2010 the tensions between North and South Korea resulted in violent clashes. In March, North Korea sank a South Korean naval ship. In response, South Korea stopped most trade with the North (although the Kaesong industries continued to operate). The attack of November 2010 followed (see pages 6–7). South Korean reactions were split. In Seoul, furious protesters demanded that their government take action after the North Korean shelling. Marine veterans (former members of the navy) staged a protest and burnt the North Korean flag. Meanwhile, opposing demonstrators protested against the joint US–South Korean live-fire military drills held near the disputed maritime border in December 2010, which they believed were a provocation to North Korea.

▲ *In April 2010 the front half of the South Korean naval ship sunk the previous month is lifted out the water.*

Case Study

South Korea's anti-base movement

▲ ***South Koreans protest against the expansion of the US military base in Pyeongtaek, 2005.***

Peace protesters form a small but vocal strand of opinion in South Korea. In the 1990s, a national movement against US military bases developed. Including activists from the peace movement, women, students and the labour movement, it demanded the reduction and eventual removal of US forces from South Korea.

Activists have strongly opposed the expansion of military bases. In 2004, a national struggle exploded against the relocation of United States Forces Korea (USFK) headquarters to Pyeongtaek. Major protests took place in 2005 and 2006. The activists aimed to attract the wider public to the cause, using art, music and street theatre to raise people's awareness. They went to Pyeongtaek and squatted (illegally occupied) the homes that had been cleared to build the base. In spring 2006, the Ministry of National Defence reacted forcefully, sending in troops to dig trenches and put up barbed wire around the perimeter. The following morning, 12,000 riot police charged in to physically remove the activists, who had barricaded themselves into a school. After this campaign, the anti-base movement declined.

Chapter 6

Confrontation or peaceful outcome?

Is there likely to be a transformation in the North Korean regime? Will there be further military conflict with the South? Is it possible to reunify Korea and how challenging would this be? This chapter considers these important questions.

Will North Korea change?

The government has introduced a few economic reforms but still restricts the markets. It regularly attempts to limit trading to older women, and certain products, such as radios and bicycles, remain restricted. The food crisis remains severe. In 2011, the country was suffering the effects of a harsh winter and a steep rise in global food prices as well as the impact of international sanctions. The government claimed that 2012 would be the year that North Korea would emerge as a prosperous nation, but without economic reform this appears unlikely. Economists have commented that gradual economic reform would be the sensible option. A sudden collapse of the state could prove disastrous.

Kim Jong-un

Leaders are not elected in North Korea. Instead, power is handed from father to son. Leader Kim Jong-il suffered a stroke in 2008; from then onwards, his son Kim Jong-un prepared to take over the leadership. Kim Jong-un was educated in Switzerland but kept away from Western influences. In February 2011, aged just 28, he was appointed vice-chairman of the National Defence Commission, the highest decision-making body in the country.

▲ *Kim Jong-un applauds at a gymnastic event, 2010.*

▲ ***On 29 April 2011 South Korean and international activists launched leaflets criticising the government into North Korea.***

Public protests

In 2011 the economic situation was so desperate that some people even took to the streets. In February, South Korean military forces dropped helium balloons containing food, medicine and radios over North Korea, along with leaflets telling them about the pro-democracy movements that had erupted in Egypt and Libya. The campaign was designed to encourage North Koreans to consider struggling for change in their country. Later in the month, a few brave North Koreans staged demonstrations against power cuts and the continuing food shortages in Jongju, Yonchon and Sonchon in North Pyongan province. They shouted, 'We can't live! Give us electricity! Give us rice!'. Yet experts on North Korea believed that these stirrings of unrest were motivated by immediate concerns about hunger rather than a desire to change the government.

Worsening North–South relations

As the situation within North Korea deteriorated, relations with the South appeared to be worsening. In February 2011, the military leaders of the two countries held a meeting to discuss the possibility of resuming negotiations. However, the North Korean delegates walked out when the two sides failed to agree on the agenda for the next round of talks.

Against this background, in February 2011, the annual joint US–South Korean military drills began. North Korea declared the exercises to be a provocation and threatened to initiate an 'all-out war' in retaliation that would turn Seoul into a 'sea of flames'. The official North Korean newspaper, the *Rodong Sinmun*, stated that 'The danger of nuclear war on the Korean peninsula is deepening.' The South Korean government claimed however that the drills had been planned for months and were not a response to the recent North Korean attacks. As of June 2011, it was unclear whether the tensions would be defused or escalate further.

Prospects for reunification

Given the heightened tensions between the two nations, what are the prospects for reuniting Korea? The challenges are huge. It would be necessary to overcome decades of suspicion to achieve unity. Even though the South Korean government expresses its

▲ ***US soldiers take part in the joint US–South Korean military exercises, March 2011.***

aim to reunite the nation, South Koreans have mixed feelings about the idea. They fear they would be overrun by millions of North Koreans seeking a better life. For many born after the Korean War, unity does not seem like an option; to them North Korea is a foreign country that they have never known.

Viewpoints:

'I do not think this particular incident [the sinking of the *Cheonan*] will escalate, but I believe that we need to have direct talks with N[orth] K[orea], and that dialogue is the best deterrence to more violence.'

Donald Gregg, 23 November 2010

- Gregg was the US ambassador to South Korea under President George H. W. Bush from 1989 to 1993. He believes that dialogue with Pyongyang is the way forward.

- Robert Gibbs was US president Barack Obama's press secretary from 2009 until February 2011. He believes North Korea needs to prove it will negotiate before talks restart.

'I think what was clear in the bilateral [two-country] talks that quickly broke down earlier this week between South Korea and North Korea was that North Korea genuinely lacked the seriousness to be involved in this. I think before we return to six-party talks, I think North Korea has to demonstrate a seriousness . . . to live up to their commitments. . . . I think they have to show a willingness to live up to their commitments and to denuclearize.'

Robert Gibbs, 11 February 2011

- Which do you think is the better approach, or is there another way?

North and South Korea: Moves towards peace

February 2007 North Korea agrees to dismantle its nuclear weapons programme in return for economic aid.

September–December 2008 Negotiations break down after North Korea starts to reassemble its nuclear plant.

July 2009 South Korea and the USA offer massive economic aid if North Korea agrees to abandon its nuclear programme; North Korea rejects the offer.

January 2011 North Korea offers talks with the South.

February 2011 Talks between the military leaders to discuss the possibility of starting new negotiations.

Reunification: costly but possible?

Some experts argue that reunification would be extremely costly for South Korea. The economic costs would be huge; estimates range from US$300 billion (£190 billion) to US$1.8 trillion (£1.1 trillion) although some experts contend that these predictions are exaggerated. Regardless of the expense, vast social differences would have to be overcome to integrate a well-educated, highly skilled population used to fast cars and all the conveniences of modern life with their impoverished neighbours. However, the few North Koreans who have escaped to the South have succeeded in making lives for themselves there, proving that it is possible to surmount the differences.

The German example

Koreans can look to the experience of Germany, which was divided into West and East Germany after World War II and reunited to become one German nation again in 1990. In that case East Germany, which had been under Communist rule and was poorer and less developed, was integrated with West Germany, a modern democratic nation. The process was hugely expensive; the eastern economy was hopelessly inefficient and the transport and communications systems required massive investment to enable economic growth. Yet overall, the reunification was successful. The divide between North and South Korea is even more extreme, yet with political will and economic muscle, reunification could still one day be within reach.

▲ *At this 2005 rally in Seoul, protesters demand the return of South Koreans who were taken prisoner during the Korean War.*

Case Study

▲ *Family reunion between relatives in North and South Korea at the North Korean resort of Mount Kumgang.*

Family reunions

Since 2000, about 21,000 South Koreans, mostly selected by lottery, have been able to meet briefly with their relatives on the other side of the border during family reunions organized by the Korean Red Cross.

Kim Dong-yul is one of them. Born in North Korea, he left Young-Heung city in 1949, hoping to return for his wife and two-year-old daughter later. But war broke out in 1950, and he was stranded in the South. In October 2010, aged 82, he was finally able to meet the daughter he had left behind. Kim Dong-yul was one of around 450 people from South Korea allowed to cross the DMZ for a family reunion in the North Korean resort of Mount Kumgang. He told the Yonhap news agency, 'I never thought it would take this long to see her again. This is the greatest moment of my life.'

Bearing a gift of underwear for his daughter (it is scarce in North Korea), Kim Dong-yul spent a few days with her before being shunted back over the border, never to see her again. Hard though this was, he was grateful for the opportunity, saying, 'I feel so sorry for those people who can't meet their loved ones. I am so lucky.'

Glossary

armistice A formal agreement during a war to stop fighting and discuss making peace.

artillery Large, heavy guns.

bio-engineering Using artificial means to assist bodily functions, such as hearing aids and false limbs.

brinkmanship In politics, entering into a dangerous situation to try to frighten people and make them do what you want.

censorship When a state or organization controls information and may prevent it from being published or broadcast.

collective farm In North Korea, a large farm owned by the government and run by a group of farmers. All the produce goes to the government, which distributes it to the people.

collectivize When the government takes over the ownership of the land and allows groups of people to farm it together.

Communist Ruled like the system of government in the former Soviet Union, where the government owned and controlled the means of production, such as farms and mines.

concession Giving up something in order to make a situation less difficult.

Confucianism A religion based on the teachings of the Chinese thinker Confucius, who lived around 500 BCE.

coup A sudden, illegal and often violent change of government.

defector To leave a country for an enemy state.

demilitarized zone An area with no military forces.

deterrent Something that is intended to stop an enemy from attack, for example, nuclear weapons.

diplomacy Managing relations between different countries.

Gross Domestic Product (GDP) The total value of all goods and services produced by a country in a year.

industrialized An industrialized country has developed industries.

juche The North Korean principle of developing in its own way and relying on its own resources rather than on other countries.

labour camp A prison camp where people are sent as a punishment; the inmates are forced to do hard labour without pay.

non-governmental organization (NGO) An organization that is not part of a government that works to help people and does not make profits.

progressive In favour of new ideas, modern methods and change.

propaganda Ideas that are often exaggerated and are used to gain support for a political system.

resolution Formal statement of opinion voted on by a group.

reunification To join together parts of a country so that they form a single nation again.

sanctions Measures imposed by a country or a group of countries to restrict trade with another nation because that nation is behaving in an unacceptable way.

shell A metal case filled with explosive to be fired from a large gun.

Soviet To do with the former Soviet Union.

Soviet Union (USSR) The former empire, ruled from Moscow in Russia, which stretched from the Baltic and Black Seas to the Pacific Ocean. It lasted from 1922 to 1991.

subsidize When a government gives money to reduce the price of producing something, for example, giving money to farmers to lower the price of food.

summit An official meeting between the leaders of two or more governments.

'sunshine policy' South Korea's policy towards North Korea from the late 1990s to 2008, which included providing support to improve relations between the two countries.

superpower A country that has great military or economic power and great influence. From 1945 until 1991, the USSR and the USA were the two superpowers.

tactical nuclear weapon A relatively small nuclear weapon designed to use in a particular battlefield in a war.

terrorism The use of violent action to try to achieve political aims.

United Nations (UN) An organization founded at the end of World War II, with the aim of preventing future wars.

Timeline

1905 Japan conquers Korea.

26 July 1945 The Potsdam Conference agrees to divide Korea into two zones.

14 November 1947 The United Nations passes a resolution calling for national elections in Korea to establish a government.

15 August 1948 The Republic of Korea is formed in the South.

9 September 1948 The Democratic People's Republic of Korea is established in the North.

25 June 1950 North Korean forces attack the South, and the Korean War begins.

27 July 1953 An armistice ends the Korean War.

16 May 1961 General Park Chung-hee takes power in South Korea in a military coup.

January 1986 North Korea's first nuclear reactor begins operation.

December 1987 Roh Tae Woo wins the South Korean elections.

December 1992 Kim Young-sam becomes the first civilian president of South Korea.

8 July 1994 Kim Il-sung dies. His son, Kim Jong-il, becomes ruler.

14 June 2000 North and South Korea sign an agreement to co-operate with each other.

15 August 2000 The first family reunions between North and South Koreans take place.

29 January 2002 US President George W. Bush declares North Korea to be part of an 'axis of evil'.

2002 The North Korean government legalizes markets.

October 2002 North Korea admits that it has a programme to produce highly enriched uranium (HEU).

27 August 2003 The Six-Party Talks begin.

2005 The USA imposes a range of financial sanctions on North Korea.

9 October 2006 North Korea tests a nuclear bomb.

13 February 2007 North Korea pledges to dismantle its nuclear weapons programme in return for economic aid.

2008 President Lee Myung-bak ends the 'sunshine policy' towards North Korea.

April 2009 North Korea pulls out of the Six-Party Talks.

Early May 2009 The North Korean government imposes price controls on non-food items in the markets.

25 May 2009 North Korea carries out a second nuclear test.

30 November 2009 North Korea devalues its currency.

2010 President Lee Myung-bak chairs the G20 group.

March 2010 North Korea sinks a South Korean naval ship, the *Cheonan*, killing 46 sailors.

23 November 2010 North Korea bombards the South Korean island of Yeonpyeong, killing four people.

December 2010 Joint US–South Korean live-fire military drills are held.

January 2011 A report to the United Nations (UN) states that North Korea has undeclared uranium enrichment facilities.

8 February 2011 The military leaders of North and South Korea hold talks to discuss the possibility of resuming negotiations.

10 February 2011 In North Korea, Kim Jong-un is appointed vice-chairman of the National Defence Commission.

14 February 2011 Protests against power cuts and food shortages take place in North Pyongang province, North Korea.

28 February 2011 Joint US–South Korean military exercises take place.

6 July 2011 The South Korean capital, Pyeongchang, is chosen as the host city for the 2018 Winter Olympic Games.

Further Information

Books

Countries in our World: South Korea by Jim Pipe (Franklin Watts, 2010)

Global Hotspots: North Korea by Clive Gifford (Macmillan Education Australia, 2011)

Facts at your Fingertips: Asia (Wayland, 2008)

Kim Jong-il's North Korea by Alison Behnke (Lerner Books, 2009)

Nothing to Envy: Real Lives in North Korea by Barbara Demick (Granta Publications, 2010)

Opposing Viewpoints: North & South Korea by Louise I. Gerdes, ed. (Thomson Gale, 2007)

Websites

Amnesty International
www.amnesty.org
Human rights organization, with reports on North and South Korea.

BBC News
www.bbc.co.uk/search/news
Has links to country profiles for North and South Korea.

CBBC
http://news.bbc.co.uk/cbbcnews/hi/newsid_2640000/newsid_2646000/2646023.stm
Guide to North Korea

Korean Central News Agency
www.kcna.co.jp
The official government-run news agency of North Korea.

Nuclear Age Peace Foundation
www.wagingpeace.org
A non-profit organization that campaigns to abolish nuclear weapons.

Index

Numbers in **bold** refer to illustrations.